cemetery dreams

t. kilgore splake

TRANSCENDENT ZERO PRESS

HOUSTON, TEXAS

PUBLISHED BY TRANSCENDENT ZERO PRESS
www.transcendentzeropress.org

ISBN-13: 978-1-946460-28-8

Printed in the United States of America

Transcendent Zero Press
16429 El Camino Real Apt. #7
Houston, TX 77062

FIRST EDITION

cemetery dreams

t. kilgore splake

Introduction
Dustin Pickering, publisher

One poet I know said Death is his constant companion. Death is the great equalizer. No matter how powerful or great your life, you will one day be regurgitated and cannibalized by the worm. splake has some premonitions of this having faced a suicide bullet during a period of dissatisfaction and existential despair.

These terse poems tell a story beyond philosophy. For instance, in "non-being" we feel that the parasitical nature of other humans, especially those closest to us, is the norm. Once in a philosophy class I was asked what do beings and non-beings have in common. After careful consideration, I suggested that the two states rely on one another. For without points of negation, nothing cannot not exist. In fact, Sartre poses this problem dialectically. Nothing must be the Ultimate.

This is splake's most philosophical collection. Using situations from his own life history, he calls back the ghosts that deaden us and puts them to work. The opening poem "rainbow heaven" reminds us why we are poets in the first place. The pain and passion sustains us. In the poem, we are the brink of sudden madness within a peaceful scene. While there is no indication of ensuing danger or irrationality, it is felt behind the scenes. Like Vonnegut, splake creates an imagistic sense of time by posing boundaries of situation. Context is everything in a fragile poetic world. This happens in Nature where the violence is really ripe. We are met with the haiku's brazen simplicity and defiance. We do not know what comes next; only premonition can speak to the reader.

I don't think the poems call others out of society into art. From an outsider's view, the entire clash of time and money is senseless. Developing meaning and purpose is far better a goal than acquiring numbers in your bank account. splake notes his relationships with young waitresses, his sense of invincibility and fearlessness, and the inevitable equality Death grants life. Throughout *Cemetery Dreams,* there is a haunted sense of invitation: you are already dead, revisiting life. Perhaps the reader is a ghost. Embracing the past without self-pity is a great feat, and splake's terse haiku-styled approach here suggests the brevity of life and the inevitability of danger throughout.

As you read these poems, consider the "cutting words" that embrace finality.

Every poet meets with Death frequently before the time comes. A poet must prepare his pillows and sheets in heaven, and earn his wings. What is it about risk that unsettles the poet and reader? In what way are these poems warning us of Death, signaling us from the shore?

Cemetery Dreams is confessional verse, purely original in its approach. These poems invite us to see what we missed when we traveled the world.

rainbow heaven

quiet stream waters
beaver dam pond
madness waiting to happen

# # # #

writing first poem

d.t.'s threatening hangover
sitting around campfire coals
waiting for meaning of life

# # # #

trees

roots in earth
branches rising to sky
seeking to touch god

# # # #

november

late night shadows
black rorschach silhouettes
breeze whispering not yet

# # # #

graybeard odyssey

slow hallway steps
down to community area
back to bedroom recliner
# # # #

with touch of honey

green tea breakfast
after many years
of bloody mary mornings
# # # #

becoming an artist

seeing and feeling
after years blinded
by credit card shine
# # # #

trout stream dreams

poet's ashes scattered
feeding wilderness worms
bait for heaven's trout
# # # #

aneurysm

brain tumor exploding
racing bloody tide
washing everything away
# # # #

bulletproof

rode bicycle without helmet
played ice hockey in wool cap
growing up unafraid
# # # #

yooper winter prayer

early 'ice out' spring
ending season of long white
god's frozen poet
# # # #

non-being

mentally ill wife
serious bi-polar girlfriend
both wanting my dreams
# # # #

becoming

meaning of life
through mother's children
world will continue
# # # #

poet

looking out hospital window
new pacemaker regular beat
praying one more year
# # # #

angry vagina

feminist confessional poet
writing about being raped
planning to kill her father
# # # #

zen surrealism

canvas creating art
artist watching palette
pushing paint brush
# # # #

plato's republic

banning all artists
for distorting truth
whitman's leaves of grass
'singing body electric'
# # # #

ghost in the shadows

knife across wrist
warm bloody flow
voices gone
no more pain
finally feeling peace
# # # #

movie goer

abandoning technicolor films
for black-and-white reality
harry lime in vienna
hank quinlan's evil touch
rosebud in flames
# # # #

carpe diem

escaping useless feelings
controlling her life
hungry important dreams
girl dying hair blue
becoming new self
# # # #

untitled

poem more important
than politician's lies
professor's lectures
monday morning workers
returning to cages
# # # #

masters of life

book learning
college classroom subjects
not describing life
beyond reference library
google computer information
reality exists
# # # #

on the edge

after night class
long three-hour lecture
first cold blue ribbon
not touching throat
like coltrane needing
dope to sustain
ecstatic high
# # # #

dear mom

sorry not obeying
your dos and don'ts
son family black sheep
forever a rolling stone
lost in muddy waters
rambling guitar blues
# # # #

brautigan creek

beside stream shadows

listening to ghost's whispers

mingling in currents

floating to dark thickets

deep in the woods

beyond cold dark water

poet going home

# # # #

reality

finding comfort

returning to nightmares

empty loneliness

existing in dark shadows

enduring constant pain

long days of nothing

better than ordinary life

# # # #

golden years

nursing home shadows

dull filmy stares

shuffling down hallways

bent over walkers

sagging wet depends

invisible ghosts

not counting anymore

# # # #

love

after husband's death

couple quickly marrying

city hall ceremony

ignoring criticisms

body not cold

lovers wisely knowing

not much time left

# # # #

mother

wrapping tuna sandwich
kitchen wax paper
bag of potato chips
hershey chocolate bar
in angler's wicker creel
young son
off on new adventure
# # # #

untitled

upper peninsula winter
season of long white
mind madly tripping
quiet whispers echoing
get out of here
like mamas and papas
california dreams
# # # #

escape

leaving bill's bible
on ymca room desk
greyhound ticket
turning square wheel miles
like ratso and joe
heading south
hungry for warm sun
cold beer waiting
# # # #

black-and-white magic

high school teenager
riviera theater film
small midwestern village
milk duds jujyfruits
hungry for manhattan
woody allen's new york
falling in love with
tracytracytracy
# # # #

mister clean

clean shaven face
suit white shirt tie
fresh shined shoes
cutting yard grass
riding lawn mower
later cleaning den
poet's writing room
dustbuster in each hand
# # # #

untitled

the brave dare
to wager their heart
roll the dice
gamble with rejection
like lottery jackpot
gold at rainbow's end
those who don't love
having nothing
# # # #

color coordinated

blue-eyed poet
pounding keyboard words
'alpha beat' keys
poems moving beyond
computer screen surface
in cold cobalt world
works never forgotten
saved somewhere forever
# # # #

november

first dawn light
waves crashing on shore
wind shaking trees
icy hard pellets
falling from gray skies
gulls bitter cry
announcing winter's
season of long white
# # # #

class reunion

quit senior year
running away from home
spending many years
looking for himself
sudden carpe diem moment
becoming a poet
now graybeard ghost
still missing in action
# # # #

feminine reality

reading used paperbacks
shopping day old bakery
buying dollar store specials
wearing thrift shop clothes
beyond seeming shallow
without latest styles
poet's new lover possessing
starving artist wisdom
# # # #

somewhere south of paradise

lost in autumn dream
time passing slowly
poet turned around
wandering two-tracks
old logging roads
forest colors still holding
enjoying fresh air
quiet peaceful moment
heading north
# # # #

blue suede shoes

singer pat boone
"april love" hit
mister nice guy
wearing white bucks
his music lost
in rock n' roll shadows
elvis loudly demanding
get yourself off my
# # # #

teenage memories

burgers and fries

dairy bar's frosted malts

jukebox in each booth

friday night sockhops

worried about zits

carrying switchblade

condom billfold circle

looking for girlfriend

unrequited love

# # # #

doing

serious driven athlete

daily pumping iron

weight room reps

waiting game's challenge

poet madly scribbling

brain bleeding ink

words filling blank page

while small little man

afraid of taking risks

nobody going nowhere

# # # #

graybeard

unlike younger poets
finding muse early in life
after writing first poem
suddenly realizing
wasting many years
making up for lost time
giving heart and mind
to creative understanding
no longer satisfied
with meaningless life
# # # #

becoming

flashlight failed
late moonless night
lost in total darkness
entire world disappearing
collapsing on path
sharp rocky trail
no longer existing
until leaving self
finally emerging
in new consciousness
# # # #

nature's art

sun moon stars

lighting the heavens

silent wilderness portrait

feathered red eagle

beautiful rainbow trout

owl's yellow eyes

deer's dark shadow

butterflies flitting

fireflies dancing

over magical canvas

# # # #

mfa bullshit

fine arts departments

graduate school classes

tenured professors

stroking entitled student egos

creating young artists

painters poets musicians

diploma certified talents

sadly not realizing

art not taught

creativity something found

# # # #

wilderness surprise

cool early morning
climbing in the cliffs
quiet day's beginning
meeting mountain lion
emerging from shadows
carefully holding breath
without any power
enjoying rare moment
sharing wild animal's trust
precious wilderness gift

# # # #

nada mas

husband at work
kids in school
maid silent shadow
bored lonely wife
buying new bracelet
another pair of shoes
happy five minutes or so
mixing valium and vodka
closing her eyes
escaping disappointing life
leaving earth behind

# # # #

hallelujah hallelujah

hungry young teenagers
high school jazz bands
practicing to become
another coltrane or 'satchmo'
move modern music
beyond duke ellington genius
like yearly mardi gras
gay festive celebration
new orleans parade
marching bands playing
'when saints come marching in'
kids and old veterans
being in that number
reaching toward heaven
hoping to touch god

# # # #

roots

mother and father
grew up on poor farms
rural church services
with hard faced minister
listening to serious sermons
telling worshippers endure
sad painful sufferings
parents now long gone
their fears still in me
nervous passing days
mad desperate feelings
living on the edge
wanting to be free

# # # #

poet's new home

no church pew
loud funeral music
tightly holding hymnal
asking sins be forgiven
praying for salvation
place in paradise
sitting beside god
upper peninsula heaven
without welcome wagon
newcomer's orientation
smoking drinking fishing
pool table contests
serious eight-ball games
poet's ghost's freedom
to fart loudly
# # # #

wildcat reflections

high school memories
being team manager
moments of celebrity
close friend of jocks
standing on sidelines
handing out towels
flirting with cheerleaders
dances and movies
dating pretty girls
not like others
debate team pussies
chess club nerds
today sadly struggling
becoming a man
lost in the shadows
sleepwalking through life
when yesterdays better

# # # #

becoming tommy

defying parents demands
about how to grow up
teenager running away
escaping military school
uniforms and morning chapel
seeking to understand life
discovering creative arts
surprised to learn
writing poems
improvising jazz riffs
choosing canvas colors
better than sex
fancy clothes wardrobe
jewelry and new cars
free of society's bullshit
driven artistic wish
chance just to be
# # # #

playing by the book

smart shy girl
sunday school regular
receiving gold star
drawing picture of jesus
church camp summers
memorizing bible passages
high school honor roll
getting all a's
on the way to college
reading books assigned
on class syllabi
writing research papers
graduate school diploma
mfa degree
worshipping professors
revered father images
believing their bullshit
rigid academic regulations
knowing nothing about life
# # # #

beyond the river

montreal shadows fading
truck's rearview mirror
turning speedometer miles
quiet early morning
following saint lawrence
passing through many
small quebec villages
gold catholic church steeples
glowing in distance
slowly sipping
warm black horse ale
lost in life's memories
top of gaspe peninsula
standing on shore
dark evening light
watching dark mists
drifting in off atlantic
poet waiting
to travel away
distant ocean tides

# # # #

pentecostal lover

after warm love making
soft pillow whispers
learning about her family
young religious childhood
like living in a cult
no television or popular music
dancing and movies
influencing sinful behaviors
halloween and harry potter
devil demon temptations
stylish clothes and jewelry
inviting evil thoughts
suggesting sex before marriage
sunday church services
worshipping jesus and god
rest of the time
important being faithful
living a blessed life
almost feeling guilty
after eating dessert
poet's new girlfriend
completely understanding
she's missed a lot
# # # #

with ghost of albert

late november afternoon
bitter saskatchewan screamer
blasting out of canada
dark silhouette shadow
leaning into the wind
slow steady steps
up snow covered trail
climbing to cliffs summit
heavy black clouds
racing across horizon
moving ahead of new storm
gathering blizzard force
strange wilderness sounds
owl's distant cry
lone coyote's howl
low dark whispers
copper miner's ghosts
trail quickly rising
snowy path bending
around shale outcropping
reaching cliffs summit
alone in open clearing
finally arriving
at end of the world
heavy grey skies
covering granite escarpment

heights vast panorama

over entire peninsula

forests spreading out below

graybeard poet answering

camus's philosophic question

choosing suicide finish

ending creative life

smith-wesson explosion

blasting bardic soul

into unknown dimensions

in quiet stillness

of solitary moment

poet suddenly possessed

by carpe diem surprise

bardic mind denying

missed past opportunities

future possible successes

instead of destroying himself

declaring time is now

deciding to return home

like tattered scarecrow

leaving farmer's field

or body of jesus

stepping down from the cross

leaving golgotha behind

hiking down from cliffs

suddenly lost in blinding snow

blizzard erasing bootprints

familiar wilderness landmarks

confidence overcoming hesitation

doubts left behind

poet no longer struggling

knowing the way

unlike "stranger" meursault

sad lost individual

without any feelings

for other people

their human existence

instead poet

getting shit together

making living worthwhile

hungry to be back writing

wrestling elusive muse

chasing creative mysteries

making sincere effort

to describe life

explain human reality

like albert camus

after fatal car crash

village of villeblevin

provence region in france

leaving behind pages

hand-written manuscript

becoming the first man

later posthumous book

graybeard's literary labors

applying beckett's wisdom

try again fail again fail better

once again enjoying

freedom to create

welcoming new becoming

# # # #